GEORGE ORWELL

PAGES FROM A
SCULLION'S DIARY

AN EXTRACT FROM 'DOWN AND OUT
IN PARIS AND LONDON'

PENGUIN BOOKS

PENGUIN BOOKS

Published by the Penguin Group. Penguin Books Ltd, 27 Wrights Lane, London w8 5tz, England. Penguin Books USA Inc., 375 Hudson Street, New York, New York 10014, USA. Penguin Books Australia Ltd, Ringwood, Victoria, Australia. Penguin Books Canada Ltd, 10 Alcorn Avenue, Toronto, Ontario, Canada m4v 3b2. Penguin Books (NZ) Ltd, 182–190 Wairau Road, Auckland 10, New Zealand · Penguin Books Ltd, Registered Offices: Harmondsworth, Middlesex, England · **This extract is taken from the edition of** *Down and Out in Paris and London* **by George Orwell that was published by Penguin Books in 1991.** This edition published 1995 · Copyright 1933 by Eric Blair. This edition copyright © the Estate of the late Sonia Brownwell Orwell, 1986. All rights reserved · Typeset by Datix International Limited, Bungay, Suffolk. Printed in England by Clays Ltd, St Ives plc · Except in the United States of America, this book is sold subject to the condition that it shall not, by way of trade or otherwise, be lent, re-sold, hired out, or otherwise circulated without the publisher's prior consent in any form of binding or cover other than that in which it is published and without a similar condition including this condition being imposed on the subsequent purchaser · 10 9 8 7 6 5 4 3 2 1

For three more days we continued traipsing about looking for work, coming home for diminishing meals of soup and bread in my bedroom. There were now two gleams of hope. In the first place, Boris had heard of a possible job at the Hôtel X, near the Place de la Concorde, and in the second, the *patron* of the new restaurant in the Rue du Commerce had at last come back. We went down in the afternoon and saw him. On the way Boris talked of the vast fortunes we should make if we got this job, and of the importance of making a good impression on the *patron*.

'Appearance – appearance is everything, *mon ami*. Give me a new suit and I will borrow a thousand francs by dinner-time. What a pity I did not buy a collar when we had money. I turned my collar inside out this morning; but what is the use, one side is as dirty as the other. Do you think I look hungry, *mon ami*?'

'You look pale.'

'Curse it, what can one do on bread and potatoes? It is fatal to look hungry. It makes people want to kick you. Wait.'

He stopped at a jeweller's window and smacked his cheeks sharply to bring the blood into them. Then, before the flush had faded, we hurried into the restaurant and introduced ourselves to the *patron*.

The *patron* was a short, fattish, very dignified man with

1

wavy grey hair, dressed in a smart double-breasted flannel suit and smelling of scent. Boris told me that he was an ex-colonel of the Russian Army. His wife was there too, a horrid fat Frenchwoman with a dead-white face and scarlet lips, reminding me of cold veal and tomatoes. The *patron* greeted Boris genially, and they talked together in Russian for a few minutes. I stood in the background, preparing to tell some big lies about my experience as a dishwasher.

Then the *patron* came over towards me. I shuffled uneasily, trying to look servile. Boris had rubbed it into me that a *plongeur* is a slave's slave, and I expected the *patron* to treat me like dirt. To my astonishment, he seized me warmly by the hand.

'So you are an Englishman!' he exclaimed. 'But how charming! I need not ask, then, whether you are a golfer?'

'*Mais certainement*,' I said, seeing that this was expected of me.

'All my life I have wanted to play golf. Will you, my dear *monsieur*, be so kind as to show me a few of the principal strokes?'

Apparently this was the Russian way of doing business. The *patron* listened attentively while I explained the difference between a driver and an iron, and then suddenly informed me that it was all *entendu*; Boris was to be *maître d'hôtel* when the restaurant opened, and I *plongeur*, with a chance of rising to lavatory attendant if trade was good. When would the restaurant open? I asked. 'Exactly a fortnight from today,' the *patron* answered grandly (he had a manner of waving his hand and flicking off his cigarette ash at the same time, which looked very grand), 'exactly a fortnight from today, in time for lunch.' Then, with obvious pride, he showed us over the restaurant.

It was a smallish place, consisting of a bar, a dining-room, and a kitchen no bigger than the average bathroom. The *patron* was decorating it in a trumpery 'picturesque' style (he called it '*normand*'; it was a matter of sham beams stuck on the plaster, and the like) and proposed to call it the Auberge de Jehan Cottard, to give a medieval effect. He had had a leaflet printed, full of lies about the historical associations of the quarter, and this leaflet actually claimed, among other things, that there had once been an inn on the site of the restaurant which was frequented by Charlemagne. The *patron* was very pleased with this touch. He was also having the bar decorated with indecent pictures by an artist from the Salon. Finally he gave us each an expensive cigarette, and after some more talk we went home.

I felt strongly that we should never get any good from this restaurant. The *patron* had looked to me like a cheat, and, what was worse, an incompetent cheat, and I had seen two unmistakable duns hanging about the back door. But Boris, seeing himself a *maître d'hôtel* once more, would not be discouraged.

'We've brought it off – only a fortnight to hold out. What is a fortnight? Food? *Je m'en fous*. To think that in only three weeks I shall have my mistress! Will she be dark or fair, I wonder? I don't mind, so long as she is not too thin.'

Two bad days followed. We had only sixty centimes left, and we spent it on half a pound of bread, with a piece of garlic to rub it with. The point of rubbing garlic on bread is that the taste lingers and gives one the illusion of having fed recently. We sat most of that day in the Jardin des Plantes. Boris had shots with stones at the tame pigeons, but always missed them, and after that we wrote dinner menus on the backs of envelopes. We were too hungry even to try and think of anything except food. I remember the dinner Boris finally selected for himself It was: a dozen oysters, borscht soup (the red, sweet, beetroot soup with cream on top), crayfishes, a young chicken *en casserole*, beef with stewed plums, new potatoes, a salad, suet pudding and Roquefort cheese, with a litre of Burgundy and some old brandy. Boris had international tastes in food. Later on, when we were prosperous, I occasionally saw him eat meals almost as large without difficulty.

When our money came to an end I stopped looking for work, and was another day without food. I did not believe that the Auberge de Jehan Cottard was really going to open, and I could see no other prospect, but I was too lazy to do anything but lie in bed. Then the luck changed abruptly. At night, at about ten o'clock, I heard an eager shout from the street. I got up and went to the window. Boris was there, waving his stick and beaming. Before speaking he dragged a bent loaf from his pocket and threw it up to me.

'*Mon ami, mon cher ami*, we're saved! What do you think?'

'Surely you haven't got a job!'

'At the Hôtel X, near the Place de la Concorde – five hundred francs a month, and food. I have been working there today. Name of Jesus Christ, how I have eaten!'

After ten or twelve hours' work, and with his game leg, his first thought had been to walk three kilometres to my hotel and tell me the good news! What was more, he told me to meet him in the Tuileries the next day during his afternoon interval, in case he should be able to steal some food for me. At the appointed time I met Boris on a public bench. He undid his waistcoat and produced a large, crushed newspaper packet; in it were some minced veal, a wedge of Camembert cheese, bread and an éclair, all jumbled together.

'*Voilà!*' said Boris, 'that's all I could smuggle out for you. The doorkeeper is a cunning swine.'

It is disagreeable to eat out of a newspaper on a public seat, especially in the Tuileries, which are generally full of pretty girls, but I was too hungry to care. While I ate, Boris explained that he was working in the *cafeterie* of the hotel – that is, in English, the stillroom. It appeared that the *cafeterie* was the very lowest post in the hotel, and a dreadful come-down for a waiter, but it would do until the Auberge de Jehan Cottard opened. Meanwhile I was to meet Boris every day in the Tuileries, and he would smuggle out as much food as he dared. For three days we continued with this arrangement, and I lived entirely on the stolen food. Then all our troubles came to an end, for one of the *plongeurs* left the Hôtel X, and on Boris's recommendation I was given a job there myself.

The Hôtel X was a vast grandiose place with a classical façade, and at one side a little dark doorway like a rat-hole, which was the service entrance. I arrived at a quarter to seven in the morning. A stream of men with greasy trousers were hurrying in and being checked by a doorkeeper who sat in a tiny office. I waited, and presently the *chef du personnel*, a sort of assistant manager, arrived and began to question me. He was an Italian, with a round, pale face, haggard from overwork. He asked whether I was an experienced dish-washer, and I said that I was; he glanced at my hands and saw that I was lying, but on hearing that I was an Englishman he changed his tone and engaged me.

'We have been looking for someone to practise our English on,' he said. 'Our clients are all Americans, and the only English we know is —' He repeated something that little boys write on the walls in London. 'You may be useful. Come downstairs.'

He led me down a winding staircase into a narrow passage, deep underground, and so low that I had to stoop in places. It was stiflingly hot and very dark, with only dim yellow bulbs several yards apart. There seemed to be miles of dark labyrinthine passages – actually, I suppose, a few hundred yards in all – that reminded one queerly of the lower decks of a liner; there were the same heat and cramped space and warm reek of food, and a humming, whirring noise (it came from the kitchen furnaces) just like the whirr of engines. We passed doorways which let out sometimes a shouting of oaths, sometimes the red glare of a fire, once a shuddering draught from an ice chamber. As we went along, something struck me violently in the back. It was a hundred-pound block of ice, carried by a blue-aproned porter. After him came a boy with a great slab of veal on his shoulder, his cheek pressed into the damp, spongy flesh. They shoved me aside with a cry of '*Range-toi, idiot!*' and rushed on. On the wall, under one of the lights, someone had written in a very neat hand: 'Sooner will you find a cloudless sky in winter, than a woman at the Hôtel X who has her maidenhead.' It seemed a queer sort of place.

One of the passages branched off into a laundry, where an old skulled-face woman gave me a blue apron and a pile of dishcloths. Then the *chef du personnel* took me to a tiny underground den – a cellar below a cellar, as it were – where there were a sink and some gas-ovens. It was too low for me to stand quite upright, and the temperature was perhaps 110 degrees Fahrenheit. The *chef du personnel* explained that my job was to fetch meals for the higher hotel employees, who fed in a small dining-room above, clean their room and wash their crockery. When he had gone, a waiter, another Italian, thrust a fierce fuzzy head into the doorway and looked down at me.

'English, eh?' he said. 'Well, I'm in charge here. If you work well' – he made the motion of up-ending a bottle and sucked noisily. 'If you don't' – he gave the doorpost several vigorous kicks. 'To me, twisting your neck would be no more than spitting on the floor. And if there's any trouble, they'll believe me, not you. So be careful.'

After this I set to work rather hurriedly. Except for about 7 an hour, I was at work from seven in the morning till a quarter past nine at night; first at washing crockery, then at scrubbing the tables and floors of the employees' dining-room, then at polishing glasses and knives, then at fetching meals, then at washing crockery again, then at fetching more meals and washing more crockery. It was easy work, and I got on well with it except when I went to the kitchen to fetch meals. The kitchen was like nothing I had ever seen or imagined – a stifling, low-ceilinged inferno of a cellar, red-lit from the fires, and deafening with oaths and the clanging of pots and pans. It was so hot that all the metal-work except the stoves had to be covered with cloth. In the middle were furnaces, where twelve cooks skipped to and fro, their faces dripping sweat in spite of their white caps. Round that were counters where a mob of waiters and *plongeurs* clamoured with trays. Scullions, naked to the waist, were stoking the fires and scouring huge copper saucepans with sand. Everyone seemed to be in a hurry and a rage. The head cook, a fine scarlet man with big moustachios, stood in the middle booming continuously, '*Ça marche, deux œufs brouillés! Ça marche, un Chateaubriand pommes sautées!*' except when he broke off to curse at a *plongeur*. There were three counters, and the first time I went to the kitchen I took my tray unknowingly to the wrong one. The head cook walked up to me, twisted his moustaches, and looked me up and down. Then he beckoned to the breakfast cook and pointed at me.

'Do you see *that*? That is the type of *plongeur* they send us nowadays. Where do you come from, idiot? From Charenton, I suppose?' (There is a large lunatic asylum at Charenton.)

'From England,' I said.

'I might have known it. Well, *mon cher monsieur l' Anglais*, may I inform you that you are the son of a whore? And now, *fous-moi le camp* to the other counter, where you belong.'

I got this kind of reception every time I went to the kitchen, for I always made some mistake; I was expected to know the work, and was cursed accordingly. From curiosity I counted the number of times I was called *maquereau* during the day, and it was thirty-nine.

At half-past four the Italian told me that I could stop working, but that it was not worth going out, as we began again at five. I went to the lavatory for a smoke; smoking was strictly forbidden, and Boris had warned me that the lavatory was the only safe place. After that I worked again till a quarter past nine, when the waiter put his head into the doorway and told me to leave the rest of the crockery. To my astonishment, after calling me pig, mackerel, etc., all day, he had suddenly grown quite friendly. I realized that the curses I had met with were only a kind of probation.

'That'll do, *mon p'tit*,' said the waiter. '*Tu n'es pas débrouillard*, but you work all right. Come up and have your dinner. The hotel allows us two litres of wine each, and I've stolen another bottle. We'll have a fine booze.'

We had an excellent dinner from the leavings of the higher employees. The waiter, grown mellow, told me stories about his love-affairs, and about two men whom he had stabbed in Italy, and about how he had dodged his military service. He was a good fellow when one got to know him; he reminded me of Benvenuto Cellini, somehow. I was tired and drenched with sweat, but I felt a new man after a day's solid food. The work did not seem difficult, and I felt that this job would suit me. It was not certain, however, that it would continue, for I had been engaged as an 'extra' for the day only, at twenty-five francs. The sour-faced doorkeeper counted out the money, less fifty centimes which he said was for insurance (a lie, I discovered afterwards). Then he stepped out into the passage, made me take off my coat, and carefully prodded me all over, searching for stolen food. After this the *chef du personnel* appeared and spoke to me. Like the waiter, he had grown more genial on seeing that I was willing to work.

'We will give you a permanent job if you like,' he said. 'The head waiter says he would enjoy calling an Englishman names. Will you sign on for a month?'

Here was a job at last, and I was ready to jump at it. Then I remembered the Russian restaurant, due to open in a fortnight. It seemed hardly fair to promise working a month, and then leave in the middle. I said that I had other work in prospect – could I be engaged for a fortnight? But at that the *chef du personnel* shrugged his shoulders and said that the hotel only engaged men by the month. Evidently I had lost my chance of a job.

Boris, by arrangement, was waiting for me in the Arcade of the Rue de Rivoli. When I told him what had happened, he was furious. For the first time since I had known him he forgot his manners and called me a fool.

'Idiot! Species of idiot! What's the good of my finding you

a job when you go and chuck it up the next moment? How could you be such a fool as to mention the other restaurant? You'd only to promise you would work for a month.'

'It seemed more honest to say I might have to leave,' I objected.

'Honest! Honest! Who ever heard of a *plongeur* being honest? *Mon ami*' – suddenly he seized my lapel and spoke very earnestly – '*mon ami*, you have worked here all day. You see what hotel work is like. Do you think a *plongeur* can afford a sense of honour?'

'No, perhaps not.'

'Well, then, go back quickly and tell the *chef du personnel* you are quite ready to work for a month. Say you will throw the other job over. Then, when our restaurant opens, we have only to walk out.'

'But what about my wages if I break my contract?'

Boris banged his stick on the pavement and cried out at such stupidity. 'Ask to be paid by the day, then you won't lose a sou. Do you suppose they would prosecute a *plongeur* for breaking his contract? A *plongeur* is too low to be prosecuted.'

I hurried back, found the *chef du personnel*, and told him that I would work for a month, whereat he signed me on. This was my first lesson in *plongeur* morality. Later I realized how foolish it had been to have any scruples, for the big hotels are quite merciless towards their employees. They engage or discharge men as the work demands, and they all sack 10 per cent or more of their staff when the season is over. Nor have they any difficulty in replacing a man who leaves at short notice, for Paris is thronged by hotel employees out of work.

As it turned out, I did not break my contract, for it was six weeks before the Auberge de Jehan Cottard even showed signs of opening. In the meantime I worked at the Hôtel X, four days a week in the *cafeterie*, one day helping the waiter on the fourth floor, and one day replacing the woman who washed up for the dining-room. My day off, luckily, was Sunday, but sometimes another man was ill and I had to work that day as well. The hours were from seven in the morning till two in the afternoon, and from five in the evening till nine – eleven hours; but it was a fourteen-hour day when I washed up for the dining-room. By the ordinary standards of a Paris *plongeur*, these are exceptionally short hours. The only hardship of the life was the fearful heat and stuffiness of those labyrinthine cellars. Apart from this the hotel, which was large and well organized, was considered a comfortable one.

Our *cafeterie* was a murky cellar measuring twenty feet by seven by eight high, and so crowded with coffee-urns, bread-cutters and the like that one could hardly move without banging against something. It was lighted by one dim electric bulb, and four or five gas-fires that sent out a fierce red breath. There was a thermometer there, and the temperature never fell below 110 degrees Fahrenheit – it neared 130 at some times of the day. At one end were five service lifts, and at the other an ice cupboard where we stored milk and butter. When you went into the ice cupboard you dropped a hundred degrees of temperature at a single step; it used to remind me of the hymn about Greenland's icy mountains and India's coral strand. Two men worked in the *cafeterie* besides Boris and myself. One was Mario, a huge, excitable Italian – he was like a city policeman with operatic gestures – and the other, a hairy, uncouth animal whom we called the Magyar; I think he was a Transylvanian, or something even more remote. Except the Magyar we were all big men, and at the rush hours we collided incessantly.

The work in the *cafeterie* was spasmodic. We were never idle, but the real work only came in bursts of two hours at a time – we called each burst '*un coup de feu*'. The first *coup de feu* came at eight, when the guests upstairs began to wake up and demand breakfast. At eight a sudden banging and yelling would break out all through the basement; bells rang on all sides, blue-aproned men rushed through the passages, our service lifts came down with a simultaneous crash, and the waiters on all five floors began shouting Italian oaths down the shafts. I don't remember all our duties, but they included making tea, coffee and chocolate, fetching meals from the kitchen, wines from the cellar, and fruit and so forth from the dining-room, slicing bread, making toast, rolling pats of butter, measuring jam, opening milk-cans, counting lumps of sugar, boiling eggs, cooking porridge, pounding ice, grinding coffee – all this for from a hundred to two hundred customers. The kitchen was thirty yards away, and the dining-room sixty or seventy yards. Everything we sent up in the service 13 lifts had to be covered by a voucher, and the vouchers had to be carefully filed, and there was trouble if even a lump of sugar was lost. Besides this, we had to supply the staff with bread and coffee, and fetch the meals for the waiters upstairs. All in all, it was a complicated job.

I calculated that one had to walk and run about fifteen miles during the day, and yet the strain of the work was more mental than physical. Nothing could be easier, on the face of it, than this stupid scullion work, but it is astonishingly hard when one is in a hurry. One has to leap to and fro between a multitude of jobs – it is like sorting a pack of cards against the clock. You are, for example, making toast, when bang! down comes a service lift with an order for tea, rolls and three different kinds of jam, and simultaneously bang! down comes another demanding scrambled eggs, coffee and grape-fruit; you run to the kitchen for the eggs and to the dining-room for the fruit, going like lightning so as to be back before your toast burns, and having to remember about the tea and coffee, besides half a dozen other orders that are still pending; and at the same time some waiter is following you and making trouble about a lost bottle of soda-water, and you are arguing with him. It needs more brains than one might think. Mario said, no doubt truly, that it took a year to make a reliable *cafetier*.

The time between eight and half-past ten was a sort of delirium. Sometimes we were going as though we had only five minutes to live; sometimes there were sudden lulls when the orders stopped and everything seemed quiet for a moment. Then we swept up the litter from the floor, threw down fresh sawdust, and swallowed gallipots of wine or coffee or water – anything, so long as it was wet. Very often we used to break off chunks of ice and suck them while we worked. The heat among the gas-fires was nauseating; we swallowed quarts of drink during the day, and after a few hours even our aprons were drenched with sweat. At times we were hopelessly behind with the work, and some of the customers would have gone without their breakfast, but Mario always pulled us through. He had worked fourteen years in the *cafeterie*, and he had the skill that never wastes a second between jobs. The Magyar was very stupid, and I was inexperienced, and Boris was inclined to shirk, partly because of his lame leg, partly because he was ashamed of working in the *cafeterie* after being a waiter; but Mario was wonderful. The way he would stretch his great arms right across the *cafeterie* to fill a coffee-pot with one hand and boil an egg with the other, at the same time watching toast and shouting directions to the Magyar, and between whiles singing snatches from *Rigoletto*, was beyond all praise. The *patron* knew his value, and he was paid a thousand francs a month, instead of five hundred like the rest of us.

The breakfast pandemonium stopped at half-past ten. Then we scrubbed the *cafeterie* tables, swept the floor and polished the brasswork, and, on good mornings, went one at a time to the lavatory for a smoke. This was our slack time – only relatively slack, however, for we had only ten minutes for lunch, and we never got through it uninterrupted. The customers' luncheon hour, between twelve and two, was another period of turmoil like the breakfast hour. Most of our work was fetching meals from the kitchen, which meant constant *engueulades* from the cooks. By this time the cooks had sweated in front of their furnaces for four or five hours, and their tempers were all warmed up.

At two we were suddenly free men. We threw off our aprons and put on our coats, hurried out of doors, and, when we had money, dived into the nearest *bistro*. It was strange, coming up into the street from those firelit cellars. The air seemed blindingly clear and cold, like arctic summer; and how sweet the petrol did smell, after the stenches of sweat and food! Sometimes we met some of our cooks and waiters in the *bistros*, and they were friendly and stood us drinks. Indoors we were their slaves, but it is an etiquette in hotel life that between hours everyone is equal, and the *engueulades* do not count.

At a quarter to five we went back to the hotel. Till half past six there were no orders, and we used this time to polish silver, clean out the coffee-urns, and do other odd jobs. Then the grand turmoil of the day started – the dinner hour. I wish I could be Zola for a little while, just to describe that dinner hour. The essence of the situation was that a hundred or two hundred people were demanding individually different meals of five or six courses, and that fifty or sixty people had to cook and serve them and clean up the mess afterwards; anyone with experience of catering will know what that means. And at this time when the work was doubled, the whole staff were tired out, and a number of them were drunk. I could write pages about the scene without giving a true idea of it. The chargings to and fro in the narrow passages, the collisions, the yells, the struggling with crates and trays and blocks of ice, the heat, the darkness, the furious festering quarrels which there was no time to fight out – they pass description. Anyone coming into the basement for the first time would have thought himself in a den of maniacs. It was only later, when I understood the working of the hotel, that I saw order in all this chaos.

At half-past eight the work stopped very suddenly. We were not free till nine, but we used to throw ourselves full length on the floor, and lie there resting our legs, too lazy even to go to the ice cupboard for a drink. Sometimes the *chef du personnel* would come in with bottles of beer, for the hotel stood us extra beer when we had had a hard day. The food we were given was no more than eatable, but the *patron* was not mean about drink; he allowed us two litres of wine a day each, knowing that if a *plongeur* is not given two litres he will steal three. We had the heeltaps of bottles as well, so that we often drank too much – a good thing, for one seemed to work faster when partially drunk.

Four days of the week passed like this; of the other two working days, one was better and one worse. After a week of this life I felt in need of a holiday. It was Saturday night, so the people in our *bistro* were busy getting drunk, and with a free day ahead of me I was ready to join them. We all went to bed, drunk, at two in the morning, meaning to sleep till noon. At half-past five I was suddenly awakened. A night-watchman, sent from the hotel, was standing at my bedside. He stripped the clothes back and shook me roughly.

'Get up!' he said. '*Tu t'es bien saoulé la gueule, pas vrai?*   17

Well, never mind that, the hotel's a man short. You've got to work today.'

'Why should I work?' I protested. 'This is my day off.'

'Day off, nothing! The work's got to be done. Get up!'

I got up and went out, feeling as though my back were broken and my skull filled with hot cinders. I did not think that I could possibly do a day's work. And yet, after only an hour in the basement, I found that I was perfectly well. It seemed that in the heat of those cellars, as in a Turkish bath, one could sweat out almost any quantity of drink. *Plongeurs* know this, and count on it. The power of swallowing quarts of wine, and then sweating it out before it can do much damage, is one of the compensations of their life.

By far my best time at the hotel was when I went to help the waiter on the fourth floor. We worked in a small pantry which communicated with the *cafeterie* by service lifts. It was delightfully cool after the cellars, and the work was chiefly polishing silver and glasses, which is a humane job. Valenti, the waiter, was a decent sort, and treated me almost as an equal when we were alone, though he had to speak roughly when there was anyone else present, for it does not do for a waiter to be friendly with *plongeurs*. He used sometimes to tip me five francs when he had had a good day. He was a comely youth, aged twenty-four but looking eighteen, and, like most waiters, he carried himself well and knew how to wear his clothes. With his black tail-coat and white tie, fresh face and sleek brown hair, he looked just like an Eton boy; yet he had earned his living since he was twelve, and worked his way up literally from the gutter. Crossing the Italian frontier without a passport, and selling chestnuts from a barrow on the northern boulevards, and being given fifty days' imprisonment in London for working without a permit, and being made love to by a rich old woman in a hotel, who gave him a diamond ring and afterwards accused him of stealing it, were among his experiences. I used to enjoy talking to him, at slack times when we sat smoking down the lift shaft.

My bad day was when I washed up for the dining-room. I had not to wash the plates, which were done in the kitchen, but only the other crockery, silver, knives and glasses; yet, even so, it meant thirteen hours' work, and I used between thirty and forty dishcloths during the day. The antiquated methods used in France double the work of washing up. Plate-racks are unheard-of, and there are no soap-flakes, only the treacly soft soap, which refuses to lather in the hard Paris water. I worked in a dirty, crowded little den, a pantry and scullery combined, which gave straight on to the dining-room. Besides washing up, I had to fetch the waiters' food and serve them at table; most of them were intolerably insolent, and I had to use my fists more than once to get common civility. The person who normally washed up was a woman, and they made her life a misery.

It was amusing to look round the filthy little scullery and think that only a double door was between us and the 19 dining-room. There sat the customers in all their splendour – spotless table-cloths, bowls of flowers, mirrors and gilt cornices and painted cherubim; and here, just a few feet away, we in our disgusting filth. For it really was disgusting filth. There was no time to sweep the floor till evening, and we slithered about in a compound of soapy water, lettuce-leaves, torn paper and trampled food. A dozen waiters with their coats off, showing their sweaty armpits, sat at the table mixing salads and sticking their thumbs into the cream pots. The room had a dirty mixed smell of food and sweat. Everywhere in the cupboards, behind the piles of crockery, were squalid stores of food that the waiters had stolen. There were only two sinks, and no washing basin, and it was nothing unusual for a waiter to wash his face in the water in which clean crockery was rinsing. But the customers saw nothing of this. There were a coconut mat and a mirror outside the dining-room door, and the waiters used to preen themselves up and go in looking the picture of cleanliness.

It is an instructive sight to see a waiter going into a hotel dining-room. As he passes the door a sudden change comes over him. The set of his shoulders alters; all the dirt and hurry and irritation have dropped off in an instant. He glides over the carpet, with a solemn priest-like air. I remember our assistant *maître d'hôtel*, a fiery Italian, pausing at the dining-room door to address an apprentice who had broken a bottle of wine. Shaking his fist above his head he yelled (luckily the door was more or less soundproof): '*Tu me fais chier*. Do you call yourself a waiter, you young bastard? You a waiter!

You're not fit to scrub floors in the brothel your mother came from. *Maquereau!*'

Words failing him, he turned to the door; and as he opened it he farted loudly, a favourite Italian insult.

Then he entered the dining-room and sailed across it dish in hand, graceful as a swan. Ten seconds later he was bowing reverently to a customer. And you could not help thinking, as you saw him bow and smile, with that benign smile of the trained waiter, that the customer was put to shame by having such an aristocrat to serve him.

This washing up was a thoroughly odious job – not hard, but boring and silly beyond words. It is dreadful to think that some people spend whole decades at such occupations. The woman whom I replaced was quite sixty years old, and she stood at the sink thirteen hours a day, six days a week, the year round; she was, in addition, horribly bullied by the waiters. She gave out that she had once been an actress – actually, I imagine, a prostitute; most prostitutes end as charwomen. It was strange to see that in spite of her age and her life she still wore a bright blonde wig, and darkened her eyes and painted her face like a girl of twenty. So apparently even a seventy-eight-hour week can leave one with some vitality.

On my third day at the hotel the *chef du personnel*, who had generally spoken to me in quite a pleasant tone, called me up and said sharply: 'Here, you, shave that moustache off at once! *Nom de Dieu*, who ever heard of a *plongeur* with a moustache?'

I began to protest, but he cut me short. 'A *plongeur* with a moustache – nonsense! Take care I don't see you with it tomorrow.'

On the way home I asked Boris what this meant. He shrugged his shoulders. 'You must do what he says, *mon ami*. No one in a hotel wears a moustache, except the cooks. I should have thought you would have noticed it. Reason? There is no reason. It is the custom.'

I saw that it was an etiquette, like not wearing a white tie with a dinner-jacket, and shaved off my moustache. Afterwards I found out the explanation of the custom, which is this: waiters in good hotels do not wear moustaches, and to show their superiority they decree that *plongeurs* shall not wear them either; and the cooks wear their moustaches to show their contempt for the waiters.

This gives some idea of the elaborate caste system existing in a hotel. Our staff, amounting to about a hundred and ten, had their prestige graded as accurately as that of soldiers, and a cook or waiter was as much above a *plongeur* as a captain above a private. Highest of all came the manager, who could sack anybody, even the cooks. We never saw the *patron*, and all we knew of him was that his meals had to be prepared more carefully than those of the customers; all the discipline of the hotel depended on the manager. He was a conscientious man, and always on the lookout for slackness, but we were too clever for him. A system of service bells ran through the hotel, and the whole staff used these for signalling to one another. A long ring and a short ring, followed by two more long rings, meant that the manager was coming, and when we heard it we took care to look busy.

Below the manager came the *maître d'hôtel*. He did not serve at table, unless to a lord or someone of that kind, but directed the other waiters and helped with the catering. His tips, and his bonus from the champagne companies (it was two francs for each cork he returned to them), came to two hundred francs a day. He was in a position quite apart from the rest of the staff, and took his meals in a private room, with silver on the table and two apprentices in clean white jackets to serve him. A little below the head waiter came the head cook, drawing about five thousand francs a month; he dined in the kitchen, but at a separate table, and one of the apprentice cooks waited on him. Then came the *chef du personnel*; he drew only fifteen hundred francs a month, but he wore a black coat and did no manual work, and he could sack *plongeurs* and fine waiters. Then came the other cooks, drawing anything between three thousand and seven hundred and fifty francs a month; then the waiters, making about seventy francs a day in tips, besides a small retaining fee; then the laundresses and sewing-women; then the apprentice waiters, who received no tips, but were paid seven hundred and fifty francs a month; then the *plongeurs*, also at seven hundred and fifty francs; then the chambermaids, at five or six hundred francs a month; and lastly the *cafetiers*, at five hundred a month. We of the *cafeterie* were the very dregs of the hotel, despised and *tutoied* by everyone.

There were various others – the office employees, called 23

generally couriers, the storekeeper, the cellarman, some porters and pages, the ice man, the bakers, the night-watchman, the doorkeeper. Different jobs were done by different races. The office employees and the cooks and sewing-women were French, the waiters Italians and Germans (there is hardly such a thing as a French waiter in Paris), the *plongeurs* of every race in Europe, besides Arabs and negroes. French was the lingua franca, even the Italians speaking it to one another.

All the departments had their special perquisites. In all Paris hotels it is the custom to sell the broken bread to bakers for eight sous a pound, and the kitchen scraps to pigkeepers for a trifle, and to divide the proceeds of this among the *plongeurs*. There was much pilfering, too. The waiters all stole food – in fact, I seldom saw a waiter trouble to eat the rations provided for him by the hotel – and the cooks did it on a larger scale in the kitchen, and we in the *cafeterie* swilled illicit tea and coffee. The cellarman stole brandy. By a rule of the hotel the waiters were not allowed to keep stores of spirits, but had to go to the cellarman for each drink as it was ordered. As the cellarman poured out the drinks he would set aside perhaps a teaspoonful from each glass, and he amassed quantities in this way. He would sell you the stolen brandy for five sous a swig if he thought he could trust you.

There were thieves among the staff, and if you left money in your coat pockets it was generally taken. The doorkeeper, who paid our wages and searched us for stolen food, was the greatest thief in the hotel. Out of my five hundred francs a month, this man actually managed to cheat me of a hundred and fourteen francs in six weeks. I had asked to be paid daily, so the doorkeeper paid me sixteen francs each evening, and, by not paying for Sundays (for which of course payment was due), pocketed sixty-four francs. Also, I sometimes worked on a Sunday, for which, though I did not know it, I was entitled to an extra twenty-five francs. The doorkeeper never paid this either, and so made away with another seventy-five francs. I only realized during my last week that I was being cheated, and, as I could prove nothing, only twenty-five francs were refunded. The doorkeeper played similar tricks on any employee who was fool enough to be taken in. He called himself a Greek, but in reality he was an Armenian. After knowing him I saw the force of the proverb 'Trust a snake before a Jew and a Jew before a Greek, but don't trust an Armenian.'

There were queer characters among the waiters. One was a gentleman – a youth who had been educated at a university, and had had a well-paid job in a business office. He had caught a venereal disease, lost his job, drifted, and now considered himself lucky to be a waiter. Many of the waiters had slipped into France without passports, and one or two of them were spies – it is a common profession for a spy to adopt. One day there was a fearful row in the waiters' dining-room between Morandi, a dangerous-looking man with eyes set too far apart, and another Italian. It appeared that Morandi had taken the other man's mistress. The other man, a weakling and obviously frightened of Morandi, was threatening vaguely.

Morandi jeered at him. 'Well, what are you going to do about it? I've slept with your girl, slept with her three times. It was fine. What can you do, eh?'

'I can denounce you to the secret police. You are an Italian spy.'

Morandi did not deny it. He simply produced a razor from his tail pocket and made two swift strokes in the air, as though slashing a man's cheeks open. Whereat the other waiter took it back.

The queerest type I ever saw in the hotel was an 'extra'. He had been engaged at twenty-five francs for the day to replace the Magyar, who was ill. He was a Serbian, a thick-set nimble fellow of about twenty-five, speaking six languages, including English. He seemed to know all about hotel work, and up till midday he worked like a slave. Then, as soon as it had struck twelve, he turned sulky, shirked his work, stole wine, and finally crowned all by loafing about openly with a pipe in his mouth. Smoking, of course, was forbidden under severe penalties. The manager himself heard of it and came down to interview the Serbian, fuming with rage.

'What the devil do you mean by smoking here?' he cried.

'What the devil do you mean by having a face like that?' answered the Serbian, calmly.

I cannot convey the blasphemy of such a remark. The head cook, if a *plongeur* had spoken to him like that, would have thrown a saucepan of hot soup in his face. The manager said instantly, 'You're sacked!' and at two o'clock the Serbian was given his twenty-five francs and duly sacked. Before he went out Boris asked him in Russian what game he was playing. He said the Serbian answered:

'Look here, *mon vieux*, they've got to pay me a day's wages if I work up to midday, haven't they? That's the law. And where's the sense of working after I get my wages? So I'll tell you what I do. I go to a hotel and get a job as an extra, and up to midday I work hard. Then, the moment it's struck twelve, I start raising such hell that they've no choice but to sack me. Neat, eh? Most days I'm sacked by half-past twelve; today it was two o'clock; but I don't care, I've saved four hours' work. The only trouble is, one can't do it at the same hotel twice.'

It appeared that he had played this game at half the hotels and restaurants in Paris. It is probably quite an easy game to play during the summer, though the hotels protect themselves against it as well as they can by means of a black list.

In a few days I had grasped the main principles on which the hotel was run. The thing that would astonish anyone coming for the first time into the service quarters of a hotel would be the fearful noise and disorder during the rush hours. It is something so different from the steady work in a shop or a factory that it looks at first sight like mere bad management. But it is really quite unavoidable, and for this reason. Hotel work is not particularly hard, but by its nature it comes in rushes and cannot be economized. You cannot, for instance, grill a steak two hours before it is wanted; you 27 have to wait till the last moment, by which time a mass of other work has accumulated, and then do it all together, in frantic haste. The result is that at meal-times everyone is doing two men's work, which is impossible without noise and quarrelling. Indeed the quarrels are a necessary part of the process, for the pace would never be kept up if everyone did not accuse everyone else of idling. It was for this reason that during the rush hours the whole staff raged and cursed like demons. At those times there was scarcely a verb in the hotel except *foutre*. A girl in the bakery, aged sixteen, used oaths that would have defeated a cabman. (Did not Hamlet say 'cursing like a scullion'? No doubt Shakespeare had watched scullions at work.) But we were not losing our heads and wasting time; we were just stimulating one another for the effort of packing four hours' work into two hours.

What keeps a hotel going is the fact that the employees take a genuine pride in their work, beastly and silly though it is. If a man idles, the others soon find him out, and conspire against him to get him sacked. Cooks, waiters and *plongeurs* differ greatly in outlook, but they are all alike in being proud of their efficiency.

Undoubtedly the most workmanlike class, and the least servile, are the cooks. They do not earn quite so much as waiters, but their prestige is higher and their employment steadier. The cook does not look upon himself as a servant, but as a skilled workman; he is generally called '*un ouvrier*', which a waiter never is. He knows his power – knows that he alone makes or mars a restaurant, and that if he is five minutes late everything is out of gear. He despises the whole non-cooking staff, and makes it a point of honour to insult everyone below the head waiter. And he takes a genuine artistic pride in his work, which demands very great skill. It is not the cooking that is so difficult, but the doing everything to time. Between breakfast and luncheon the head cook at the Hôtel X would receive orders for several hundred dishes, all to be served at different times; he cooked few of them himself, but he gave instructions about all of them and inspected them before they were sent up. His memory was wonderful. The vouchers were pinned on a board, but the head cook seldom looked at them; everything was stored in his mind, and exactly to the minute, as each dish fell due, he would call out, '*Faites marcher une côtelette de veau*' (or whatever it was) unfailingly. He was an insufferable bully, but he was also an artist. It is for their punctuality, and not for any superiority in technique, that men cooks are preferred to women.

The waiter's outlook is quite different. He too is proud in a way of his skill, but his skill is chiefly in being servile. His work gives him the mentality, not of a workman, but of a snob. He lives perpetually in sight of rich people, stands at their tables, listens to their conversation, sucks up to them with smiles and discreet little jokes. He has the pleasure of spending money by proxy. Moreover, there is always the chance that he may become rich himself, for, though most waiters die poor, they have long runs of luck occasionally. At some cafés on the Grand Boulevard there is so much money to be made that the waiters actually pay the *patron* for their employment. The result is that between constantly seeing money, and hoping to get it, the waiter comes to identify himself to some extent with his employers. He will take pains to serve a meal in style, because he feels that he is participating in the meal himself.

I remember Valenti telling me of some banquet at Nice at which he had once served, and of how it cost two hundred thousand francs and was talked of for months afterwards. 'It was splendid, *mon p'tit, mais magnifique*! Jesus Christ! The champagne, the silver, the orchids – I have never seen anything like them, and I have seen some things. Ah, it was glorious!'

'But,' I said, 'you were only there to wait?'

'Oh, of course. But still, it was splendid.'

The moral is, never be sorry for a waiter. Sometimes when you sit in a restaurant, still stuffing yourself half an hour after closing time, you feel that the tired waiter at your side must surely be despising you. But he is not. He is not thinking as he looks at you, 'What an overfed lout'; he is thinking, 'One day, when I have saved enough money, I shall be able to imitate that man.' He is ministering to a kind of pleasure he thoroughly understands and admires. And that is why waiters are seldom Socialists, have no effective trade union, and will work twelve hours a day – they work fifteen hours, seven days a week, in many cafés. They are snobs, and they find the servile nature of their work rather congenial.

The *plongeurs*, again, have a different outlook. Theirs is a
job which offers no prospects, is intensely exhausting, and at

the same time has not a trace of skill or interest; the sort of job that would always be done by women if women were strong enough. All that is required of them is to be constantly on the run, and to put up with long hours and a stuffy atmosphere. They have no way of escaping from this life, for they cannot save a penny from their wages, and working from sixty to a hundred hours a week leaves them no time to train for anything else. The best they can hope is to find a slightly softer job as night-watchman or lavatory attendant.

And yet the *plongeurs*, low as they are, also have a kind of pride. It is the pride of the drudge – the man who is equal to no matter what quantity of work. At that level, the mere power to go on working like an ox is about the only virtue attainable. *Débrouillard* is what every *plongeur* wants to be called. A *débrouillard* is a man who, even when he is told to do the impossible, will *se débrouiller* – get it done somehow. One of the kitchen *plongeurs* at the Hôtel X, a German, was well known as a *débrouillard*. One night an English lord came to the hotel, and the waiters were in despair, for the lord had asked for peaches, and there were none in stock; it was late at night, and the shops would be shut. 'Leave it to me,' said the German. He went out, and in ten minutes he was back with four peaches. He had gone into a neighbouring restaurant and stolen them. That is what is meant by a *débrouillard*. The English lord paid for the peaches at twenty francs each.

Mario, who was in charge of the *cafeterie*, had the typical drudge mentality. All he thought of was getting through the '*boulot*', and he defied you to give him too much of it. 31

Fourteen years underground had left him with about as much natural laziness as a piston rod. '*Faut être un dur*,' he used to say when anyone complained. You will often hear *plongeurs* boast, '*Je suis un dur*' as though they were soldiers, not male charwomen.

Thus everyone in the hotel had his sense of honour, and when the press of work came we were all ready for a grand concerted effort to get through it. The constant war between the different departments also made for efficiency, for everyone clung to his own privileges and tried to stop the others idling and pilfering.

This is the good side of hotel work. In a hotel a huge and complicated machine is kept running by an inadequate staff, because every man has a well-defined job and does it scrupulously. But there is a weak point, and it is this – that the job the staff are doing is not necessarily what the customer pays for. The customer pays, as he sees it, for good service; the employee is paid, as he sees it, for the *boulot* – meaning, as a rule, an imitation of good service. The result is that, though hotels are miracles of punctuality, they are worse than the worst private houses in the things that matter.

Take cleanliness, for example. The dirt in the Hôtel X, as soon as one penetrated into the service quarters, was revolting. Our *cafeterie* had year-old filth in all the dark corners, and the bread-bin was infested with cockroaches. Once I suggested killing these beasts to Mario. 'Why kill the poor animals?' he said reproachfully. The others laughed when I wanted to wash my hands before touching the butter. Yet we were clean where we recognized cleanliness as part of the *boulot*. We scrubbed the tables and polished the brasswork regularly, because we had orders to do that; but we had no orders to be genuinely clean, and in any case we had no time for it. We were simply carrying out our duties; and as our first duty was punctuality, we saved time by being dirty.

In the kitchen the dirt was worse. It is not a figure of speech, it is a mere statement of fact to say that a French cook will spit in the soup – that is, if he is not going to drink it himself. He is an artist, but his art is not cleanliness. To a certain extent he is even dirty because he is an artist, for food, to look smart, needs dirty treatment. When a steak, for instance, is brought up for the head cook's inspection, he does not handle it with a fork. He picks it up in his fingers and slaps it down, runs his thumb round the dish and licks it to taste the gravy, runs it round and licks it again, then steps back and contemplates the piece of meat like an artist judging a picture, then presses it lovingly into place with his fat, pink fingers, every one of which he has licked a hundred times that morning. When he is satisfied, he takes a cloth and wipes his fingerprints from the dish, and hands it to the waiter. And the waiter, of course, dips *his* fingers into the gravy – his nasty, greasy fingers which he is for ever running through his brilliantined hair. Whenever one pays more than, say, ten francs for a dish of meat in Paris, one may be certain that it has been fingered in this manner. In very cheap restaurants it is different; there, the same trouble is not taken over the food, and it is just forked out of the pan and flung on to a plate, without handling. Roughly speaking, the more 33 one pays for food, the more sweat and spittle one is obliged to eat with it.

Dirtiness is inherent in hotels and restaurants, because sound food is sacrificed to punctuality and smartness. The hotel employee is too busy getting food ready to remember that it is meant to be eaten. A meal is simply '*une commande*' to him, just as a man dying of cancer is simply 'a case' to the doctor. A customer orders, for example, a piece of toast. Somebody, pressed with work in a cellar deep underground, has to prepare it. How can he stop and say to himself 'This toast is to be eaten – I must make it eatable'? All he knows is that it must look right and must be ready in three minutes. Some large drops of sweat fall from his forehead on to the toast. Why should he worry? Presently the toast falls among the filthy sawdust on the floor. Why trouble to make a new piece? It is much quicker to wipe the sawdust off. On the way upstairs the toast falls again, butter side down. Another wipe is all it needs. And so with everything. The only food at the Hôtel X which was ever prepared cleanly was the staff's, and the *patron*'s. The maxim, repeated by everyone, was: 'Look out for the *patron*, and as for the clients, *s'en fout pas mal!*' Everywhere in the service quarters dirt festered – a secret vein of dirt, running through the great garish hotel like the intestines through a man's body.

Apart from the dirt, the *patron* swindled the customers wholeheartedly. For the most part the materials of the food were very bad, though the cooks knew how to serve it up in style. The meat was at best ordinary, and as to the vegetables, no good housekeeper would have looked at them in the market. The cream, by a standing order, was diluted with milk. The tea and coffee were of inferior sorts, and the jam was synthetic stuff out of vast unlabelled tins. All the cheaper wines, according to Boris, were corked *vin ordinaire*. There was a rule that employees must pay for anything they spoiled, and in consequence damaged things were seldom thrown away. Once the waiter on the third floor dropped a roast chicken down the shaft of our service lift, where it fell into a litter of broken bread, torn paper and so forth at the bottom. We simply wiped it with a cloth and sent it up again. Upstairs there were dirty tales of once-used sheets not being washed, but simply damped, ironed and put back on the beds. The *patron* was as mean to us as to the customers. Throughout that vast hotel there was not, for instance, such a thing as a brush and pan; one had to manage with a broom and a piece of cardboard. And the staff lavatory was worthy of Central Asia, and there was no place to wash one's hands, except the sinks used for washing crockery.

In spite of all this the Hôtel X was one of the dozen most expensive hotels in Paris, and the customers paid startling prices. The ordinary charge for a night's lodging, not including breakfast, was two hundred francs. All wine and tobacco were sold at exactly double shop prices, though of course the *patron* bought at the wholesale price. If a customer had a title, or was reputed to be a millionaire, all his charges went up automatically. One morning on the fourth floor an American who was on diet wanted only salt and hot water for his breakfast. Valenti was furious. 'Jesus Christ!' he said, 'what about my ten per cent? Ten per cent of salt and water!' 35

And he charged twenty-five francs for the breakfast. The customer paid without a murmur.

According to Boris, the same kind of thing went on in all Paris hotels, or at least in all the big, expensive ones. But I imagine that the customers at the Hôtel X were especially easy to swindle, for they were mostly Americans, with a sprinkling of English – no French – and seemed to know nothing whatever about good food. They would stuff themselves with disgusting American 'cereals', and eat marmalade at tea, and drink vermouth after dinner, and order a *poulet à la reine* at a hundred francs and then souse it in Worcester sauce. One customer, from Pittsburg, dined every night in his bedroom on grape-nuts, scrambled eggs and cocoa. Perhaps it hardly matters whether such people are swindled or not.

I heard queer tales in the hotel. There were tales of dope fiends, of old debauchees who frequented hotels in search of pretty page-boys, of thefts and blackmail. Mario told me of a hotel in which he had been, where a chambermaid stole a priceless diamond ring from an American lady. For days the staff were searched as they left work, and two detectives searched the hotel from top to bottom, but the ring was never found. The chambermaid had a lover in the bakery, and he had baked the ring into a roll, where it lay unsuspected until the search was over.

Once Valenti, at a slack time, told me a story about himself.

'You know, *mon p'tit*, this hotel life is all very well, but it's the devil when you're out of work. I expect you know what it is to go without eating, eh? *Forcément*, otherwise you wouldn't be scrubbing dishes. Well, I'm not a poor devil of a *plongeur*; I'm a waiter, and *I* went five days without eating, once. Five days without even a crust of bread – Jesus Christ!

'I tell you, those five days were the devil. The only good thing was, I had my rent paid in advance. I was living in a dirty, cheap little hotel in the Rue Sainte-Éloïse up in the Latin quarter. It was called the Hôtel —, after some famous prostitute who was born in that quarter, I expect. I was starving, and there was nothing I could do; I couldn't even go to the cafés where the hotel proprietors come to engage waiters, because I hadn't the price of a drink. All I could do was to lie in bed getting weaker and weaker, and watching the bugs running about the ceiling. I don't want to go through that again, I can tell you.

'In the afternoon of the fifth day I went half mad; at least, that's how it seems to me now. There was an old faded print of a woman's head hanging on the wall of my room, and I took to wondering who it could be; and after about an hour I realized that it must be Sainte Éloïse, who was the patron saint of the quarter. I had never taken any notice of the thing before, but now, as I lay staring at it, a most extraordinary idea came into my head.

'"*Écoute, mon cher*," I said to myself, "you'll be starving to death if this goes on much longer. You've got to do something. Why not try a prayer to Sainte Éloïse? Go down on your knees and ask her to send you some money. After all, it can't do any harm. Try it!"

37

'Mad, eh? Still, a man will do anything when he's hungry. Besides, as I said, it couldn't do any harm. I got out of bed and began praying. I said:

'"Dear Sainte Éloïse, if you exist, please send me some money. I don't ask for much – just enough to buy some bread and a bottle of wine and get my strength back. Three or four francs would do. You don't know how grateful I'll be, Sainte Éloïse, if you help me this once. And be sure, if you send me anything, the first thing I'll do will be to go and burn a candle for you, at your church down the street. Amen."

'I put in that about the candle, because I had heard that saints like having candles burnt in their honour. I meant to keep my promise, of course. But I am an atheist and I didn't really believe that anything would come of it.

'Well, I got into bed again, and five minutes later there came a bang at the door. It was a girl called Maria, a big fat peasant girl who lived at our hotel. She was a very stupid girl, but a good sort, and I didn't much care for her to see me in the state I was in.

'She cried out at the sight of me. "*Nom de Dieu!*" she said, "what's the matter with you? What are you doing in bed at this time of day? *T'en as une mine!* You look more like a corpse than a man."

'Probably I did look a sight. I had been five days without food, most of the time in bed, and it was three days since I had had a wash or a shave. The room was a regular pigsty, too.

38   '"What's the matter?" said Maria again.

'"The matter!" I said; "Jesus Christ! I'm starving. I haven't eaten for five days. That's what's the matter."

'Maria was horrified. "Not eaten for five days?" she said. "But why? Haven't you any money, then?"

'"Money!" I said. "Do you suppose I should be starving if I had money? I've got just five sous in the world, and I've pawned everything. Look round the room and see if there's anything more I can sell or pawn. If you can find anything that will fetch fifty centimes, you're cleverer than I am."

'Maria began looking round the room. She poked here and there among a lot of rubbish that was lying about, and then suddenly she got quite excited. Her great thick mouth fell open with astonishment.

'"You idiot!" she cried out. "Imbecile! What's *this*, then?"

'I saw that she had picked up an empty oil *bidon* that had been lying in the corner. I had bought it weeks before, for an oil lamp I had before I sold my things.

'"That?" I said. "That's an oil *bidon*. What about it?"

'"Imbecile! Didn't you pay three francs fifty deposit on it?"

'Now, of course I had paid the three francs fifty. They always make you pay a deposit on the *bidon*, and you get it back when the *bidon* is returned. But I'd forgotten all about it.

'"Yes—" I began.

'"Idiot!" shouted Maria again. She got so excited that she began to dance about until I thought her sabots would go through the floor. "Idiot! *T'es louf! T'es louf!* What have you got to do but take it back to the shop and get your deposit back? Starving, with three francs fifty staring you in the face! Imbecile!"

'I can hardly believe now that in all those five days I had never once thought of taking the *bidon* back to the shop. As good as three francs fifty in hard cash, and it had never occurred to me! I sat up in bed. "Quick!" I shouted to Maria, "you take it for me. Take it to the grocer's at the corner – run like the devil. And bring back food!"

'Maria didn't need to be told. She grabbed the *bidon* and went clattering down the stairs like a herd of elephants, and in three minutes she was back with two pounds of bread under one arm and a half-litre bottle of wine under the other. I didn't stop to thank her; I just seized the bread and sank my teeth in it. Have you noticed how bread tastes when you have been hungry for a long time? Cold, wet, doughy – like putty almost. But, Jesus Christ, how good it was! As for the wine, I sucked it all down in one draught, and it seemed to go straight into my veins and flow round my body like new blood. Ah, that made a difference!

'I wolfed the whole two pounds of bread without stopping to take breath. Maria stood with her hands on her hips, watching me eat. "Well, you feel better, eh?" she said when I had finished.

'"Better!" I said. "I feel perfect! I'm not the same man as I was five minutes ago. There's only one thing in the world I need now – a cigarette."

'Maria put her hand in her apron pocket. "You can't have

it," she said. "I've no money. This is all I had left out of your three francs fifty – seven sous. It's no good; the cheapest cigarettes are twelve sous a packet."

'"Then I can have them!" I said. "Jesus Christ, what a piece of luck! I've got five sous – it's just enough."

'Maria took the twelve sous and was starting out to the tobacconist's. And then something I had forgotten all this time came into my head. There was that cursed Sainte Éloïse! I had promised her a candle if she sent me money; and really, who could say that the prayer hadn't come true? "Three or four francs," I had said; and the next moment along came three francs fifty. There was no getting away from it. I should have to spend my twelve sous on a candle.

'I called Maria back. "It's no use," I said; "there is Sainte Éloïse – I have promised her a candle. The twelve sous will have to go on that. Silly, isn't it? I can't have my cigarettes after all."

'"Sainte Éloïse?" said Maria. "What about Sainte Éloïse?"

'"I prayed to her for money and promised her a candle," I said. "She answered the prayer – at any rate, the money turned up. I shall have to buy that candle. It's a nuisance, but it seems to me I must keep my promise."

'"But what put Sainte Éloïse into your head?" said Maria.

'"It was her picture," I said, and I explained the whole thing. "There she is, you see," I said, and I pointed to the picture on the wall.

'Maria looked at the picture, and then to my surprise she burst into shouts of laughter. She laughed more and more, stamping about the room and holding her fat sides as though 41 they would burst. I thought she had gone mad. It was two minutes before she could speak.

'"Idiot!" she cried at last. "*T'es louf! T'es louf!* Do you mean to tell me you really knelt down and prayed to that picture? Who told you it was Sainte Éloïse?"

'"But I made sure it was Sainte Éloïse!" I said.

'"Imbecile! It isn't Sainte Éloïse at all. Who do you think it is?"

'"Who?" I said.

'"It is —, the woman this hotel is called after."

'I had been praying to —, the famous prostitute of the Empire . . .

'But, after all, I wasn't sorry. Maria and I had a good laugh, and then we talked it over, and we made out that I didn't owe Sainte Éloïse anything. Clearly it wasn't she who had answered the prayer, and there was no need to buy her a candle. So I had my packet of cigarettes after all.'

Time went on and the Auberge de Jehan Cottard showed no signs of opening. Boris and I went down there one day during our afternoon interval and found that none of the alterations had been done, except the indecent pictures, and there were three duns instead of two. The *patron* greeted us with his usual blandness, and the next instant turned to me (his prospective dishwasher) and borrowed five francs. After that I felt certain that the restaurant would never get beyond talk. The *patron*, however, again named the opening for 'exactly a fortnight from today', and introduced us to the woman who was to do the cooking, a Baltic Russian five feet tall and a yard across the hips. She told us that she had been a singer before she came down to cooking, and that she was very artistic and adored English literature, especially *La Case de l'Oncle Tom*.

In a fortnight I had got so used to the routine of a *plongeur*'s life that I could hardly imagine anything different. It was a life without much vacation. At a quarter to six one woke with a sudden start, tumbled into grease-stiffened clothes, and hurried out with dirty face and protesting muscles. It was dawn, and the windows were dark except for the workmen's cafés. The sky was like a vast flat wall of cobalt, with roofs and spires of black paper pasted upon it. Drowsy men were sweeping the pavements with ten-foot besoms, and ragged families picking over the dustbins. Workmen, and girls with a piece of chocolate in one hand and a *croissant* in the other, were pouring into the Metro stations. Trams, filled with more workmen, boomed gloomily past. One hastened down to the station, fought for a place – one does literally have to fight on the Paris Metro at six in the morning – and stood jammed in the swaying mass of passengers, nose to nose with some hideous French face, breathing sour wine and garlic. And then one descended into the labyrinth of the hotel basement, and forgot daylight till two o'clock, when the sun was hot and the town black with people and cars.

After my first week at the hotel I always spent the afternoon interval in sleeping, or, when I had money, in a *bistro*. Except for a few ambitious waiters who went to English classes, the 43 whole staff wasted their leisure in this way; one seemed too lazy after the morning's work to do anything better. Sometimes half a dozen *plongeurs* would make up a party and go to an abominable brothel in the Rue de Sieyès, where the charge was only five francs twenty-five centimes – tenpence half-penny. It was nicknamed '*le prix fixe*,' and they used to describe their experiences there as a great joke. It was a favourite rendezvous of hotel workers. The *plongeurs*' wages did not allow them to marry, and no doubt work in the basement does not encourage fastidious feelings.

For another four hours one was in the cellars, and then one emerged, sweating, into the cool street. It was lamplight – that strange purplish gleam of the Paris lamps – and beyond the river the Eiffel Tower flashed from top to bottom with zigzag skysigns, like enormous snakes of fire. Streams of cars glided silently to and fro, and women, exquisite-looking in the dim light, strolled up and down the arcade. Sometimes a woman would glance at Boris or me, and then, noticing our greasy clothes, look hastily away again. One fought another battle in the Metro and was home by ten. Generally from ten to midnight I went to a little *bistro* in our street, an underground place frequented by Arab navvies. It was a bad place for fights, and I sometimes saw bottles thrown, once with fearful effect, but as a rule the Arabs fought among themselves and let Christians alone. *Raki*, the Arab drink, was very cheap, and the *bistro* was open at all hours, for the Arabs – lucky men – had the power of working all day and drinking all night.

44   It was the typical life of a *plongeur*, and it did not seem a

bad life at the time. I had no sensation of poverty, for even after paying my rent and setting aside enough for tobacco and journeys and my food on Sundays, I still had four francs a day for drinks, and four francs was wealth. There was – it is hard to express it – a sort of heavy contentment, the contentment a well-fed beast might feel, in a life which had become so simple. For nothing could be simpler than the life of a *plongeur*. He lives in a rhythm between work and sleep, without time to think, hardly conscious of the exterior world; his Paris has shrunk to the hotel, the Metro, a few *bistros* and his bed. If he goes afield, it is only a few streets away, on a trip with some servant-girl who sits on his knee swallowing oysters and beer. On his free day he lies in bed till noon, puts on a clean shirt, throws dice for drinks, and after lunch goes back to bed again. Nothing is quite real to him but the *boulot*, drinks and sleep; and of these sleep is the most important.

One night, in the small hours, there was a murder just beneath my window. I was woken by a fearful uproar, and, going to the window, saw a man lying flat on the stones below; I could see the murderers, three of them, flitting away at the end of the street. Some of us went down and found that the man was quite dead, his skull cracked with a piece of lead piping. I remember the colour of his blood, curiously purple, like wine; it was still on the cobbles when I came home that evening, and they said the schoolchildren had come from miles round to see it. But the thing that strikes me in looking back is that I was in bed and asleep within three minutes of the murder. So were most of the people in the street; we just made sure that the man was done for, and went straight back to bed. We were working people, and where was the sense of wasting sleep over a murder?

Work in the hotel taught me the true value of sleep, just as being hungry had taught me the true value of food. Sleep had ceased to be a mere physical necessity; it was something voluptuous, a debauch more than a relief. I had no more trouble with the bugs. Mario had told me of a sure remedy for them, namely pepper, strewed thick over the bedclothes. It made me sneeze, but the bugs all hated it, and emigrated to other rooms.

With thirty francs a week to spend on drinks I could take part in the social life of the quarter. We had some jolly evenings, on Saturdays, in the little *bistro* at the foot of the Hôtel des Trois Moineaux.

The brick-floored room, fifteen feet square, was packed with twenty people, and the air dim with smoke. The noise was deafening, for everyone was either talking at the top of his voice or singing. Sometimes it was just a confused din of voices; sometimes everyone would burst out together in the same song – the 'Marseillaise', or the 'Internationale', or 'Madelon', or 'Les Fraises et les Framboises'. Azaya, a great clumping peasant girl who worked fourteen hours a day in a glass factory, sang a song about, '*Elle a perdu son pantalon, tout en dansant le Charleston.*' Her friend Marinette, a thin, dark Corsican girl of obstinate virtue, tied her knees together and danced the *danse du ventre*. The old Rougiers wandered in and out, cadging drinks and trying to tell a long, involved story about someone who had once cheated them over a bedstead. R., cadaverous and silent, sat in his corner quietly boozing. Charlie, drunk, half danced, half staggered to and fro with a glass of sham absinthe balanced in one fat hand, pinching the women's breasts and declaiming poetry. People played darts and diced for drinks. Manuel, a Spaniard, dragged the girls to the bar and shook the dice-box against their bellies, for luck. Madame F. stood at the bar rapidly pouring *chopines* of wine through the pewter funnel, with a wet dishcloth always handy, because every man in the room tried to make love to her. Two children, bastards of big Louis the bricklayer, sat in a corner sharing a glass of *sirop*. Everyone was very happy, overwhelmingly certain that the world was a good place and we a notable set of people.

For an hour the noise scarcely slackened. Then about midnight there was a piercing shout of '*Citoyens!*' and the sound of a chair falling over. A blond, red-faced workman had risen to his feet and was banging a bottle on the table. Everyone stopped singing; the word went round, 'Sh! Fureux is starting!' Fureux was a strange creature, a Limousin stone-mason who worked steadily all the week and drank himself into a kind of paroxysm on Saturdays. He had lost his memory and could not remember anything before the war, and he would have gone to pieces through drink if Madame F. had not taken care of him. On Saturday evenings at about five o'clock she would say to someone, 'Catch Fureux before he spends his wages,' and when he had been caught she would take away his money, leaving him enough for one good drunk. One week he escaped, and, rolling blind drunk in the Place Monge, was run over by a car and badly hurt.

The queer thing about Fureux was that, though he was a Communist when sober, he turned violently patriotic when drunk. He started the evening with good Communist principles, but after four or five litres he was a rampant Chauvinist, denouncing spies, challenging all foreigners to fight, and, if he was not prevented, throwing bottles. It was at this stage that he made his speech – for he made a patriotic speech every Saturday night. The speech was always the same, word for word. It ran:

'Citizens of the Republic, are there any Frenchmen here? If there are any Frenchmen here, I rise to remind them – to remind them in effect, of the glorious days of the war. When one looks back upon that time of comradeship and heroism – one looks back, in effect, upon that time of comradeship and heroism. When one remembers the heroes who are dead – one remembers, in effect, the heroes who are dead. Citizens of the Republic, I was wounded at Verdun—'

Here he partially undressed and showed the wound he had received at Verdun. There were shouts of applause. We thought nothing in the world could be funnier than this speech of Fureux's. He was a well-known spectacle in the quarter; people used to come in from other *bistros* to watch him when his fit started.

The word was passed round to bait Fureux. With a wink to the others someone called for silence, and asked him to
sing the 'Marseillaise'. He sang it well, in a fine bass voice,

with patriotic gurgling noises deep down in his chest when he came to '*Aux arrmes, citoyens! Forrmez vos bataillons!*' Veritable tears rolled down his cheeks; he was too drunk to see that everyone was laughing at him. Then, before he had finished, two strong workmen seized him by either arm and held him down, while Azaya shouted, '*Vive l' Allemagne!*' just out of his reach. Fureux's face went purple at such infamy. Everyone in the *bistro* began shouting together, '*Vive l' Allemagne! À bas la France!*' while Fureux struggled to get at them. But suddenly he spoiled the fun. His face turned pale and doleful, his limbs went limp, and before anyone could stop him he was sick on the table. Then Madame F. hoisted him like a sack and carried him up to bed. In the morning he reappeared, quiet and civil, and bought a copy of *L'Humanité*.

The table was wiped with a cloth, Madame F. brought more litre bottles and loaves of bread, and we settled down to serious drinking. There were more songs. An itinerant singer came in with his banjo and performed for five-sou pieces. An Arab and a girl from the *bistro* down the street did a dance, the man wielding a painted wooden phallus the size of a rolling-pin. There were gaps in the noise now. People had begun to talk about their love-affairs, and the war, and the barbel fishing in the Seine, and the best way to *faire la révolution*, and to tell stories. Charlie, grown sober again, captured the conversation and talked about his soul for five minutes. The doors and windows were opened to cool the room. The street was emptying, and in the distance one could hear the lonely milk train thundering down the

Boulevard St-Michel. The air blew cold on our foreheads, and the coarse African wine still tasted good; we were still happy, but meditatively, with the shouting and hilarious mood finished.

By one o'clock we were not happy any longer. We felt the joy of the evening wearing thin, and called hastily for more bottles, but Madame F. was watering the wine now, and it did not taste the same. Men grew quarrelsome. The girls were violently kissed and hands thrust into their bosoms and they made off lest worse should happen. Big Louis, the bricklayer, was drunk, and crawled about the floor barking and pretending to be a dog. The others grew tired of him and kicked at him as he went past. People seized each other by the arm and began long rambling confessions, and were angry when these were not listened to. The crowd thinned. Manuel and another man, both gamblers, went across to the Arab *bistro*, where card-playing went on till daylight. Charlie suddenly borrowed thirty francs from Madame F. and disappeared, probably to a brothel. Men began to empty their glasses, call briefly, ''sieurs, dames!' and go off to bed.

By half-past one the last drop of pleasure had evaporated, leaving nothing but headaches. We perceived that we were not splendid inhabitants of a splendid world, but a crew of underpaid workmen grown squalidly and dismally drunk. We went on swallowing the wine, but it was only from habit, and the stuff seemed suddenly nauseating. One's head had swollen up like a balloon, the floor rocked, one's tongue and lips were stained purple. At last it was no use keeping it up any longer.

Several men went out into the yard behind the *bistro* and were sick. We crawled up to bed, tumbled down half dressed, and stayed there ten hours.

Most of my Saturday nights went in this way. On the whole, the two hours when one was perfectly and wildly happy seemed worth the subsequent headache. For many men in the quarter, unmarried and with no future to think of, the weekly drinking-bout was the one thing that made life worth living.

Charlie told us a good story one Saturday night in the *bistro*. Try and picture him – drunk, but sober enough to talk consecutively. He bangs on the zinc bar and yells for silence:

'Silence, *messieurs et dames* – silence, I implore you! Listen to this story that I am about to tell you. A memorable story, an instructive story, one of the souvenirs of a refined and civilized life. Silence, *messieurs et dames!*

'It happened at a time when I was hard up. You know what that is like – how damnable, that a man of refinement should ever be in such a condition. My money had not come from home; I had pawned everything, and there was nothing open to me except to work, which is a thing I will not do. I was living with a girl at the time – Yvonne her name was – a great half-witted peasant girl like Azaya there, with yellow hair and fat legs. The two of us had eaten nothing in three days. *Mon Dieu*, what sufferings! The girl used to walk up 51 and down the room with her hands on her belly, howling like a dog that she was dying of starvation. It was terrible.

'But to a man of intelligence nothing is impossible. I propounded to myself the question, "What is the easiest way to get money without working?" And immediately the answer came: "To get money easily one must be a woman. Has not every woman something to sell?" And then, as I lay reflecting upon the things I should do if I were a woman, an idea came into my head. I remembered the Government maternity hospitals – you know the Government maternity hospitals? They are places where women who are *enceinte* are given meals free and no questions are asked. It is done to encourage childbearing. Any woman can go there and demand a meal, and she is given it immediately.

'"*Mon Dieu!*" I thought, "if only I were a woman! I would eat at one of those places every day. Who can tell whether a woman is *enceinte* or not, without an examination?"

'I turned to Yvonne. "Stop that insufferable bawling," I said; "I have thought of a way to get food."

'"How?" said she.

'"It is simple," I said. "Go to the Government maternity hospital. Tell them you are *enceinte* and ask for food. They will give you a good meal and ask no questions."

'Yvonne was appalled. "*Mais, mon Dieu*," she cried, "I am not *enceinte*!"

'"Who cares?" I said. "That is easily remedied. What do you need except a cushion – two cushions if necessary? It is an inspiration from heaven, *ma chère*. Don't waste it."

'Well, in the end I persuaded her, and then we borrowed a cushion and I got her ready and took her to the maternity hospital. They received her with open arms. They gave her cabbage soup, a ragoût of beef, a purée of potatoes, bread and cheese and beer, and all kinds of advice about her baby. Yvonne gorged till she almost burst her skin, and managed to slip some of the bread and cheese into her pocket for me. I took her there every day until I had money again. My intelligence had saved us.

'Everything went well until a year later. I was with Yvonne again, and one day we were walking down the Boulevard Port Royal, near the barracks. Suddenly Yvonne's mouth fell open, and she began turning red and white, and red again.

'"*Mon Dieu!*" she cried, "look at that who is coming! It is the nurse who was in charge at the maternity hospital. I am ruined!"

'"Quick!" I said, "run!" But it was too late. The nurse had recognized Yvonne, and she came straight up to us, smiling. She was a big fat woman with a gold pince-nez and red cheeks like the cheeks of an apple. A motherly, interfering kind of woman.

'"I hope you are well, *ma petite*?" she said kindly. "And your baby, is he well too? Was it a boy, as you were hoping?"

'Yvonne had begun trembling so hard that I had to grip her arm. "No," she said at last.

'"Ah, then, *évidemment*, it was a girl?"

'Thereupon Yvonne, the idiot, lost her head completely. "No," she actually said again!

'The nurse was taken aback. "*Comment!*" she exclaimed, "neither a boy nor a girl! But how can that be?"

'Figure to yourselves, *messieurs et dames*, it was a dangerous moment. Yvonne had turned the colour of a beetroot and looked ready to burst into tears; another second and she would have confessed everything. Heaven knows what might have happened. But as for me, I had kept my head; I stepped in and saved the situation.

'"It was twins," I said calmly.

'"Twins!" exclaimed the nurse. And she was so pleased that she took Yvonne by the shoulders and embraced her on both cheeks, publicly.

'Yes, twins . . .'

MARTIN AMIS · *God's Dice*
HANS CHRISTIAN ANDERSEN · *The Emperor's New Clothes*
MARCUS AURELIUS · *Meditations*
JAMES BALDWIN · *Sonny's Blues*
AMBROSE BIERCE · *An Occurrence at Owl Creek Bridge*
DIRK BOGARDE · *From Le Pigeonnier*
WILLIAM BOYD · *Killing Lizards*
POPPY Z. BRITE · *His Mouth will Taste of Wormwood*
ITALO CALVINO · *Ten Italian Folktales*
ALBERT CAMUS · *Summer*
TRUMAN CAPOTE · *First and Last*
RAYMOND CHANDLER · *Goldfish*
ANTON CHEKHOV · *The Black Monk*
ROALD DAHL · *Lamb to the Slaughter*
ELIZABETH DAVID · *I'll be with You in the Squeezing of a Lemon*
N. J. DAWOOD (TRANS.) · *The Seven Voyages of Sindbad the Sailor*
ISAK DINESEN · *The Dreaming Child*
SIR ARTHUR CONAN DOYLE · *The Man with the Twisted Lip*
DICK FRANCIS · *Racing Classics*
SIGMUND FREUD · *Five Lectures on Psycho-Analysis*
KAHLIL GIBRAN · *Prophet, Madman, Wanderer*
STEPHEN JAY GOULD · *Adam's Navel*
ALASDAIR GRAY · *Five Letters from an Eastern Empire*
GRAHAM GREENE · *Under the Garden*
JAMES HERRIOT · *Seven Yorkshire Tales*
PATRICIA HIGHSMITH · *Little Tales of Misogyny*
M. R. JAMES AND R. L. STEVENSON · *The Haunted Dolls' House*
RUDYARD KIPLING · *Baa Baa, Black Sheep*
PENELOPE LIVELY · *A Long Night at Abu Simbel*
KATHERINE MANSFIELD · *The Escape*

PENGUIN 60s